Valtopia
An Expansive Coloring Journey

Created by Val Cripps

Printed in the United States of America

First Printing, 2015

ISBN 978-1519277299

ISBN-10: 1519277296

www.Valtopia.com · www.facebook.com/groups/Valtopia/

Dedication

First, I dedicate this book to my brother, David Berney, who is no longer with us on this plane. He is most definitely with me in spirit, and I know I wouldn't have evolved and expanded as I have over the last year without his spiritual presence. Every circle you see in the book, you can think of him and send love to all the souls who are "too sensitive" for this world. Sensitivity is a super power, and the world is coming into this truth. May you all recognize your special sensitivities and honor and develop what you are especially tuned into. You are a gift of the universe.

To all of my lovely family, here in America and in England, I appreciate and love you. To my husband who has experienced a super Valtopian transformation and jumped in to support and help make this project see completion, thank you. Without you I'd still be editing and dreading dealing with getting to print!! You are a vastly spiritual, expansive, kind, patient and gifted man, and we are blessed to have created our gorgeous family together. To our boys, John and Charlie, who give me magic cuddles every day and who will light up the world with their brilliance and love. To my lovely mother who always encouraged us to dream, be kind, and set a powerful example of spiritual expansion and to cherish the most humble and daily of life's moments. To my dad, so vital and exuberant, who allowed me to explore my powerful and ambitious self from a very early age, motivating me to go for the gusto and do the best I can do. Thank you both for trusting and supporting me and always loving me. To my aunt Barbara, who gifted me sophisticated and professional artist tools from the very youngest age, and who prepared me for all this tracing with my light table as a kid! Thank you for advising and guiding me with your graphic design wisdom, experience and love and for always being there for me, especially now to help me design and finish this book! To all my angel sisters and magical Valtopians, your energy from near and far, virtually and behind the scenes, has been absolutely vital to me and I'm ever grateful and joyful for your presence and love. Thank you, Hilary Sperling Stauffer for the beautiful professional photos you captured of me. Thank you Tish Hicks, Adele Cabot, Randina Marie, and Becky Kimes for inspiring me on my spiritual journey and continuing to nurture me all along the way with so much love and vision, and to all my soul sisters who I love dearly and look forward to experiencing with you, so much more love and light. And to all future Valtopians, such radiant sunshine lies ahead of us.

Welcome

Welcome to Valtopia. We are so grateful you are taking time for yourself to relax and zen out. Life seems to get so busy, and the more we rush and fuss, though we think we might be getting more done, we can really sabotage the best of ourselves. In our experience, the more time we take to get calm, get grounded, and really dream and energize ourselves, the more our dreams come true.

At the back of the book, you'll find a guide to each image, with an inspirational bit of wisdom and guidance to think about as you color. The energy imbued in the images is yours to receive, should you be open. The experience is yours, and there are some open spaces in the drawings to allow your mind spontaneous creativity as your spirit leads you. Color by yourself, or color with those you love and explore the ideas and thoughts and feelings that come up. Be free and doodle what you feel. If you don't want to color, you can always trace the images! Tracing these provides a powerfully calming and focusing effect that can really zone you in.

Accompanying each image are suggestions of crystals and essential oils that can assist and support you in your expansive journey. What we visualize and think about becomes our truth and our reality! Dream big, dream strong and make it happen.

As an artist, I would like to recommend the tools that I enjoy using to color in my drawings. I am a HUGE fan of Prismacolor pencils. If you press lightly and draw little circles, you can get a base layer of color. Then when you press firmly, the pencils have a rich, waxy consistency that creates a deep and vibrant color that pops. For markers, you want to find a nice fine tipped marker like Staedtler or Sharpie. You can even get some black ink pens and draw over some of the lines after you have colored in with color. Enjoy!!

Want to join the Valtopia community and meet like minded spirits who will bolster and support you? Find us online at Valtopia.com and on Facebook at www.facebook.com/groups/ Valtopia/. Thank you for joining us and for buying and enjoying this coloring book. You are now officially a Valtopian!

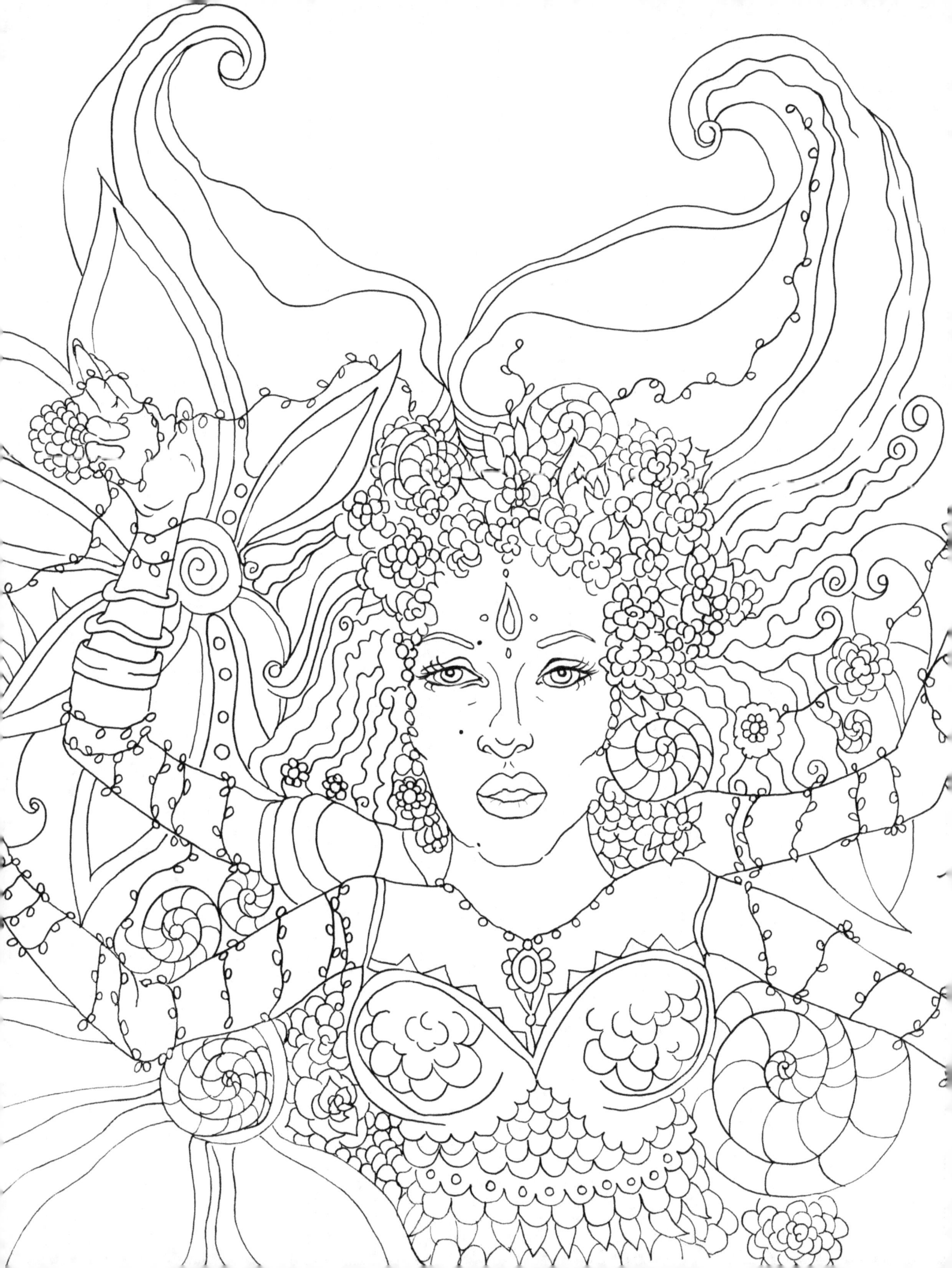

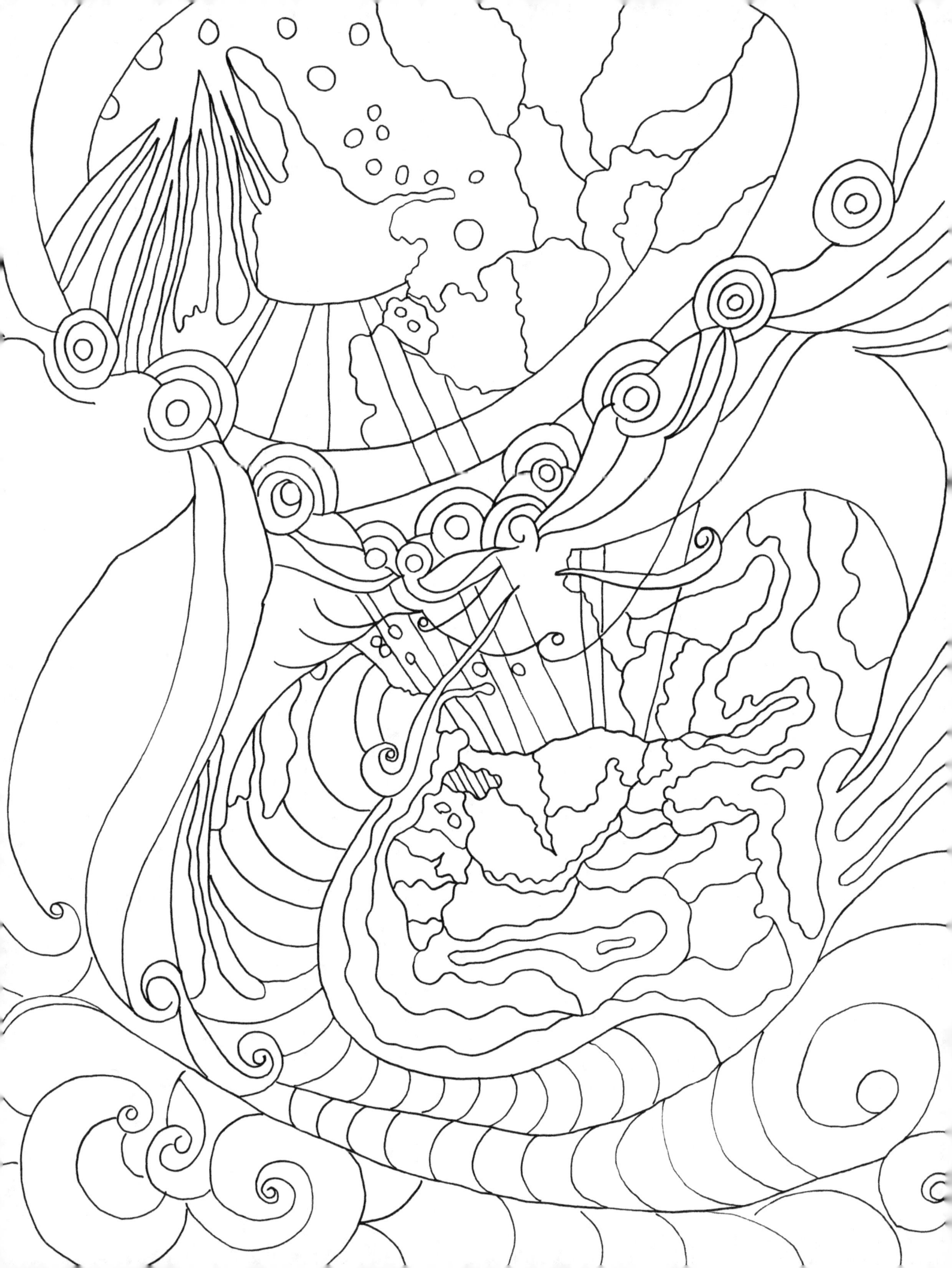

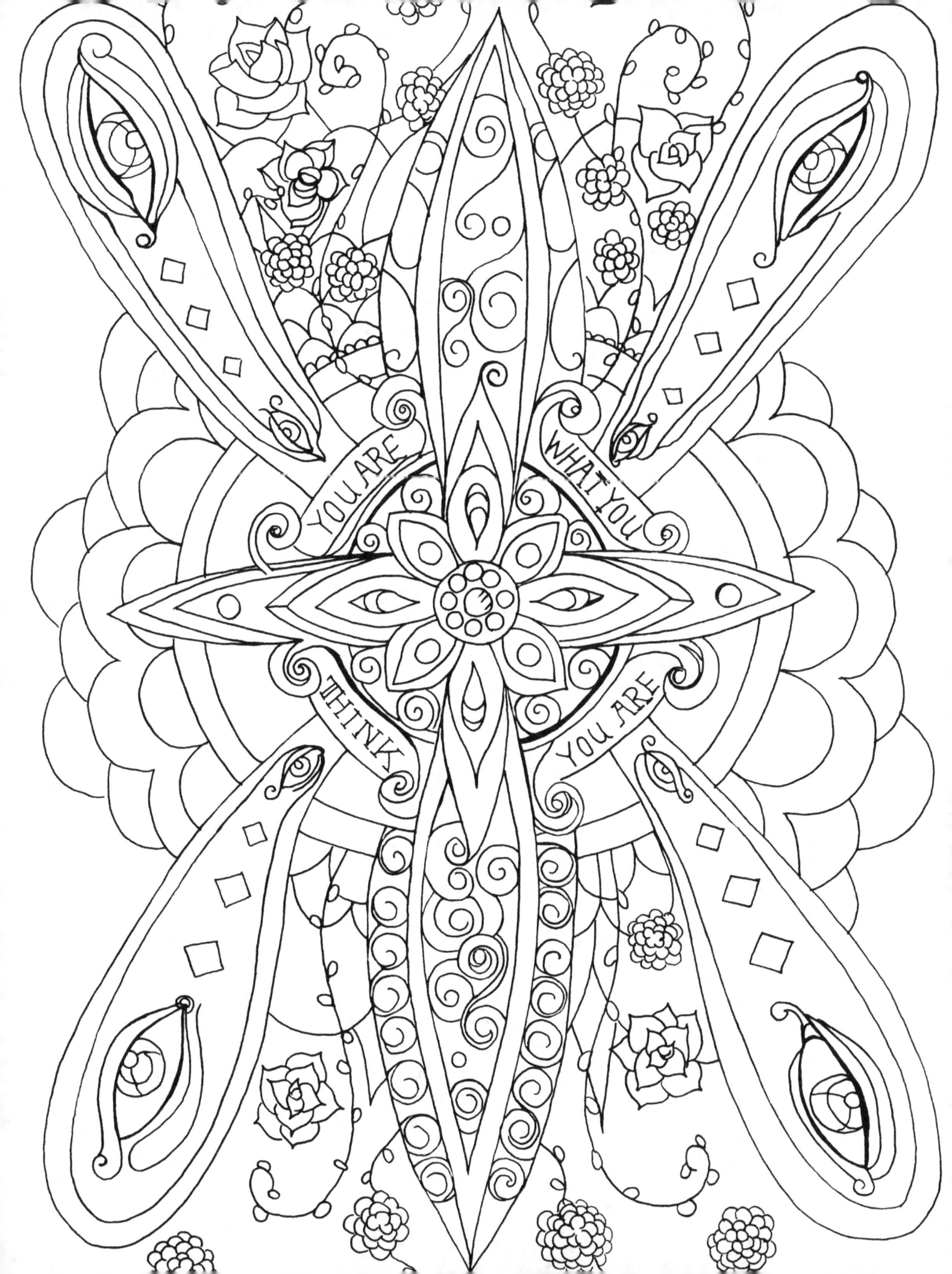

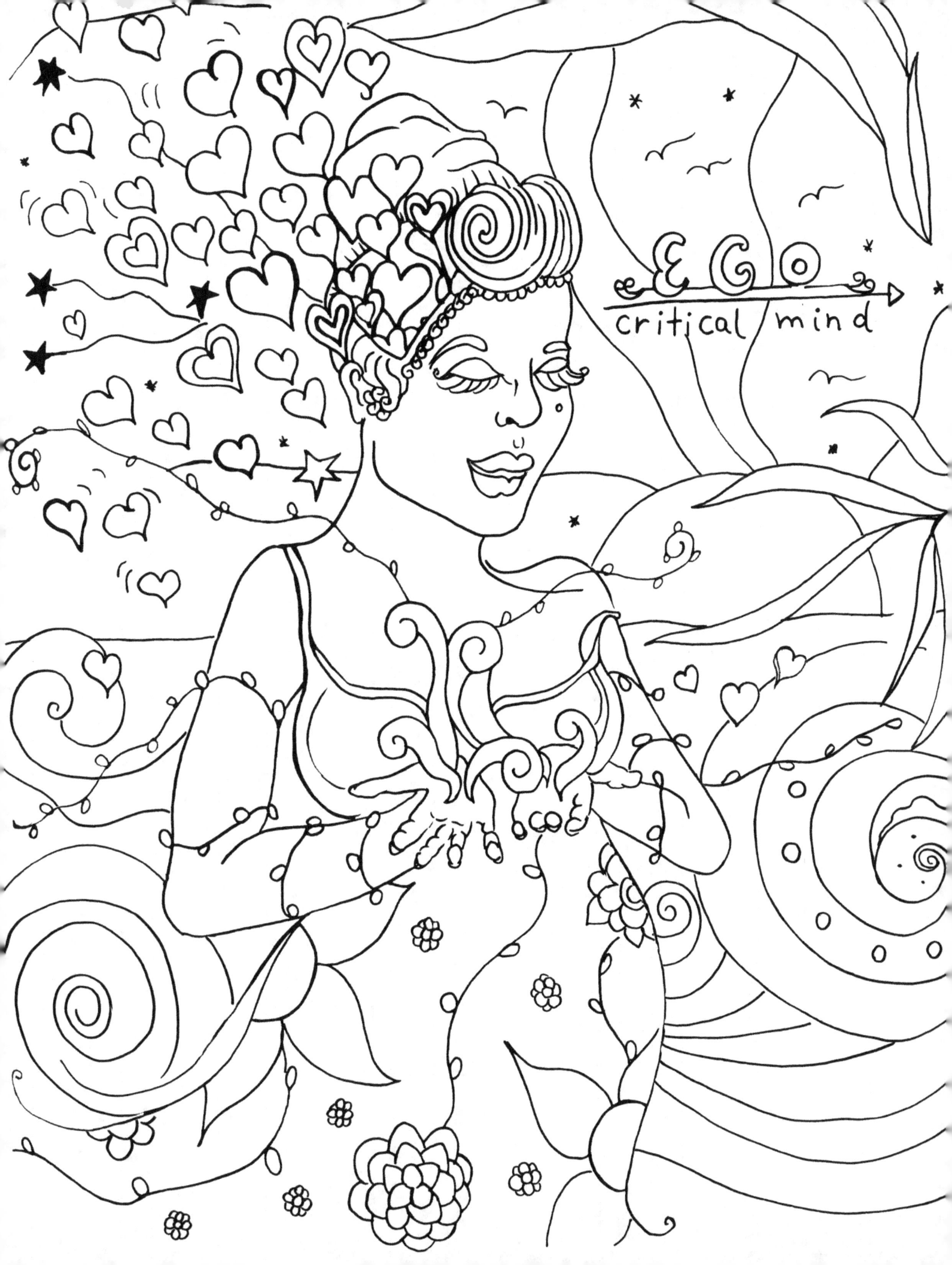

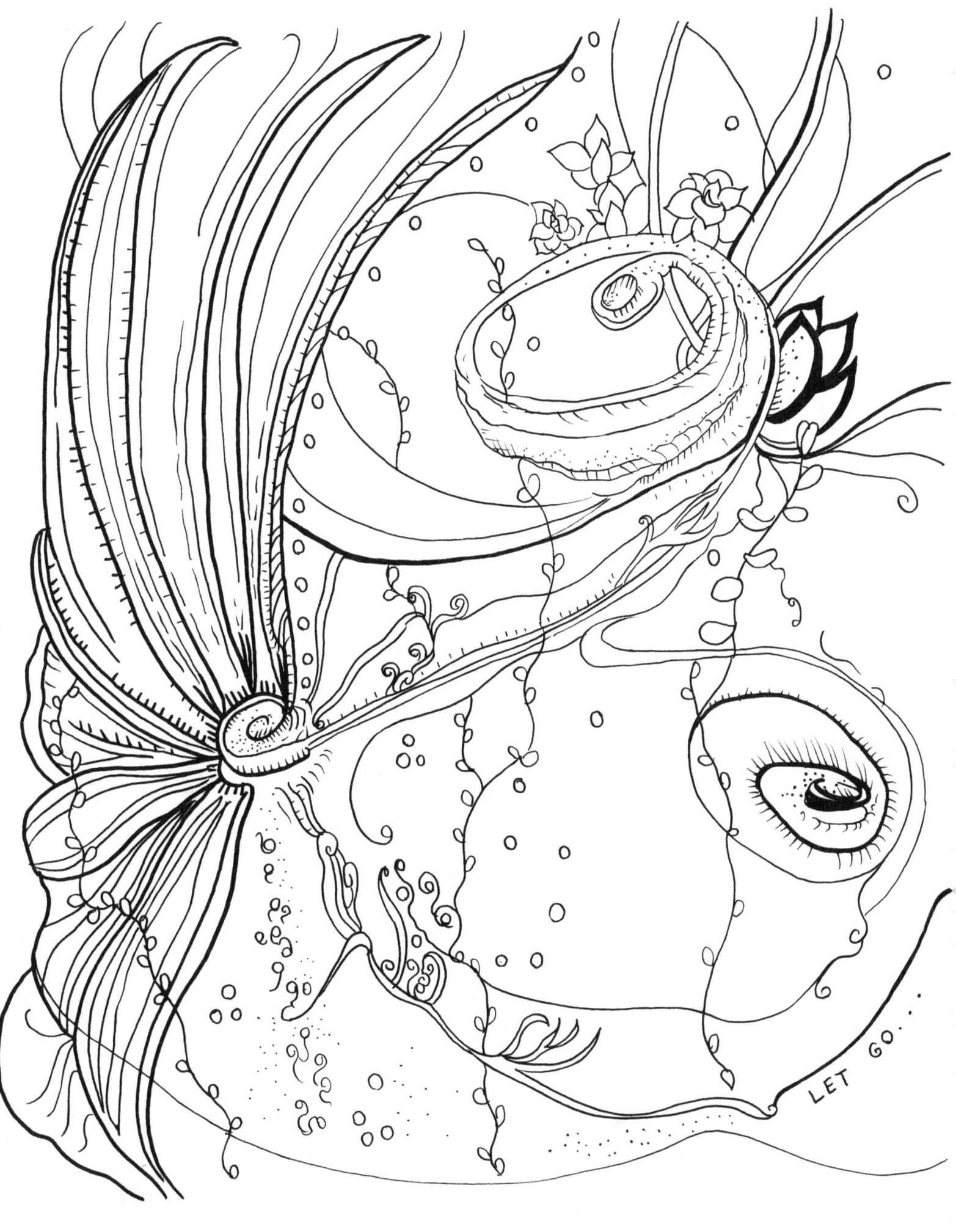

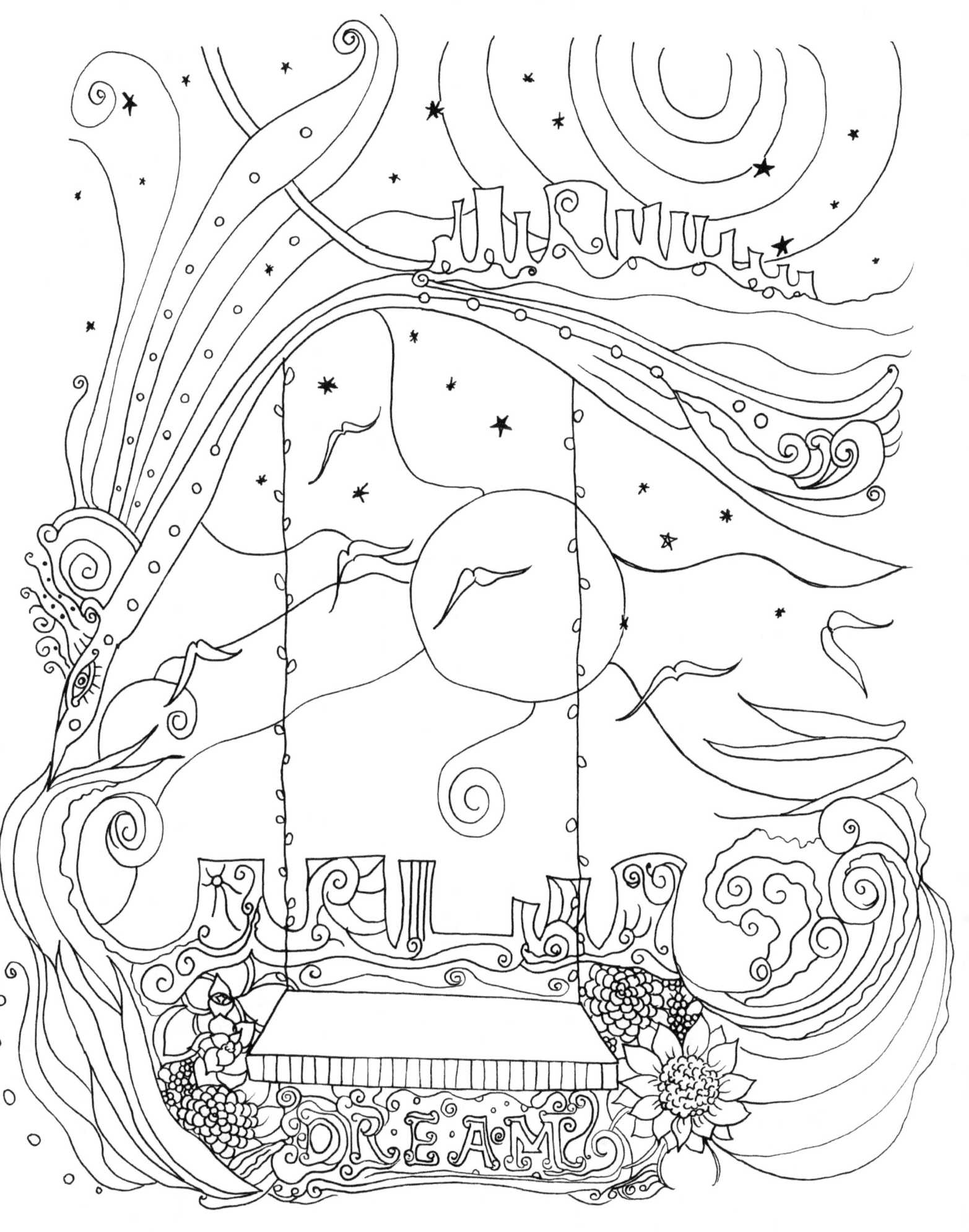

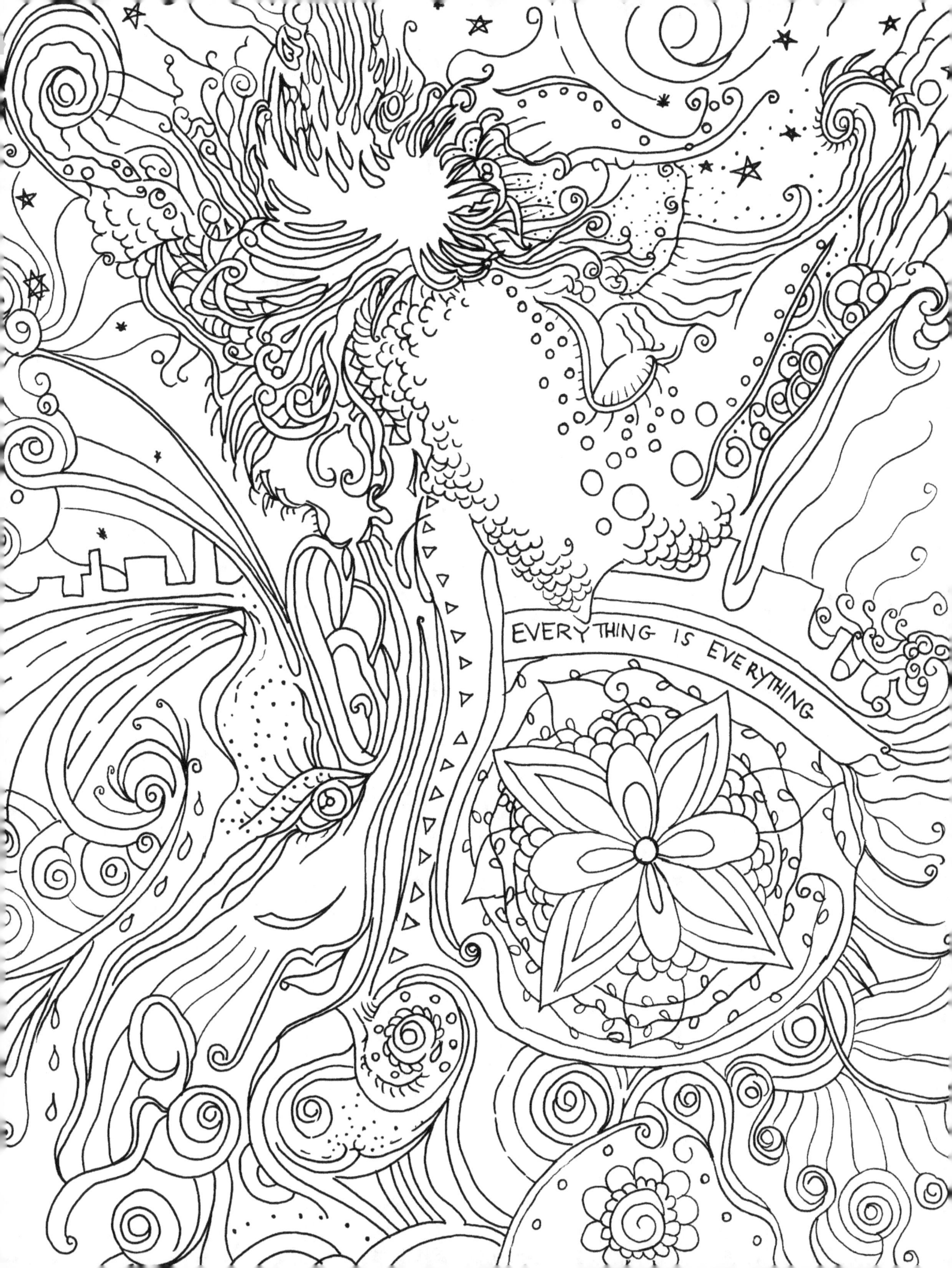

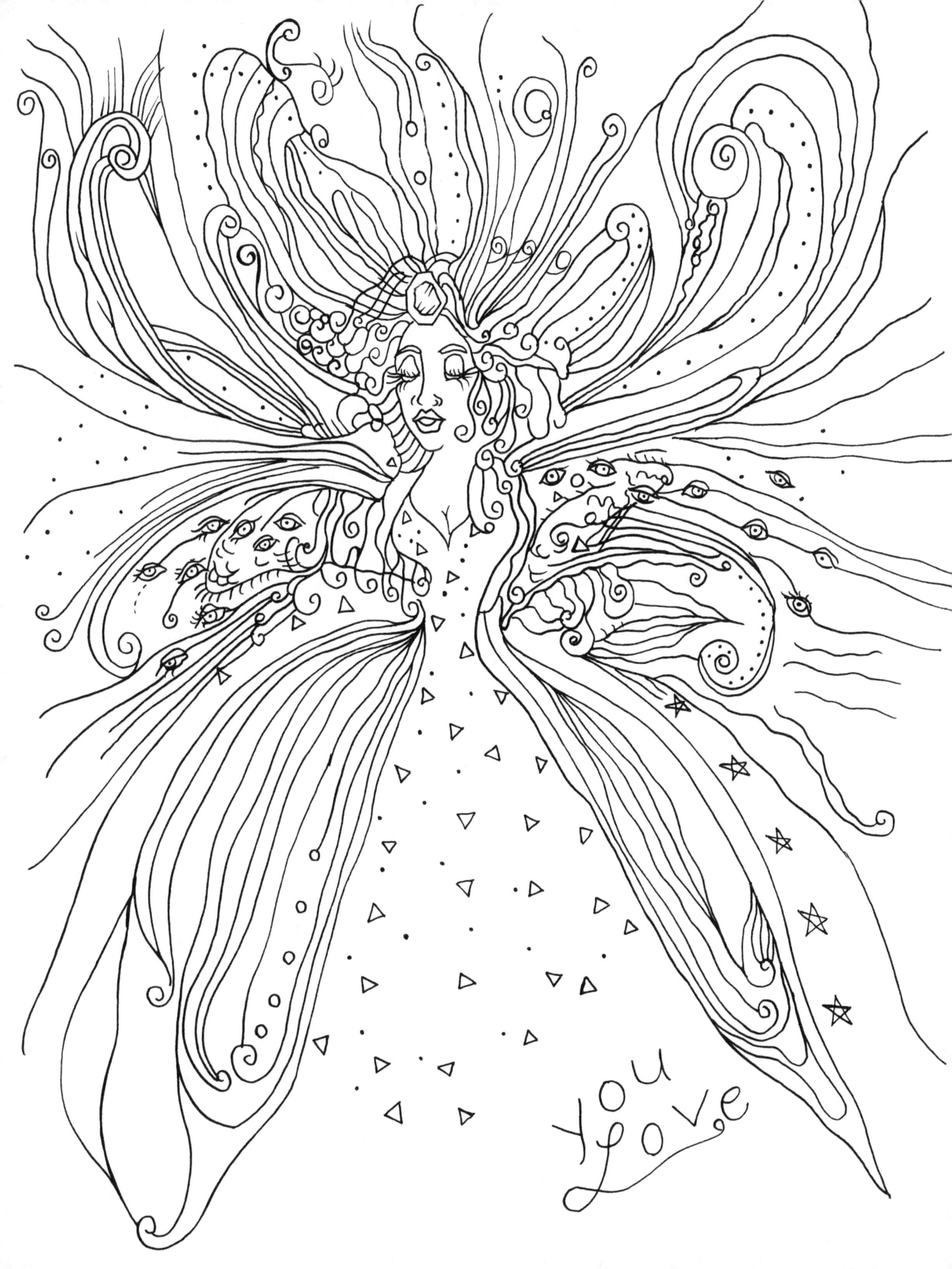

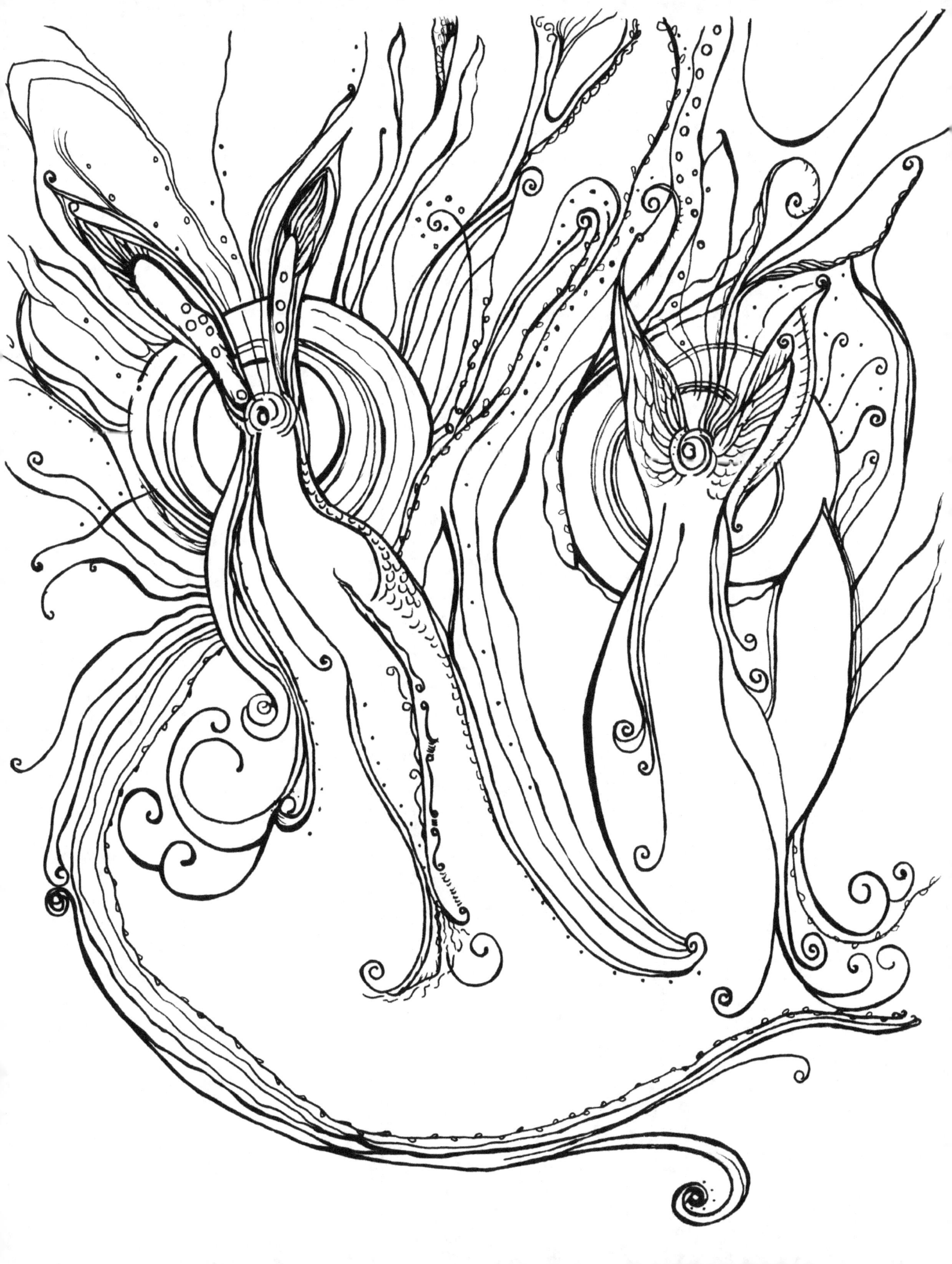

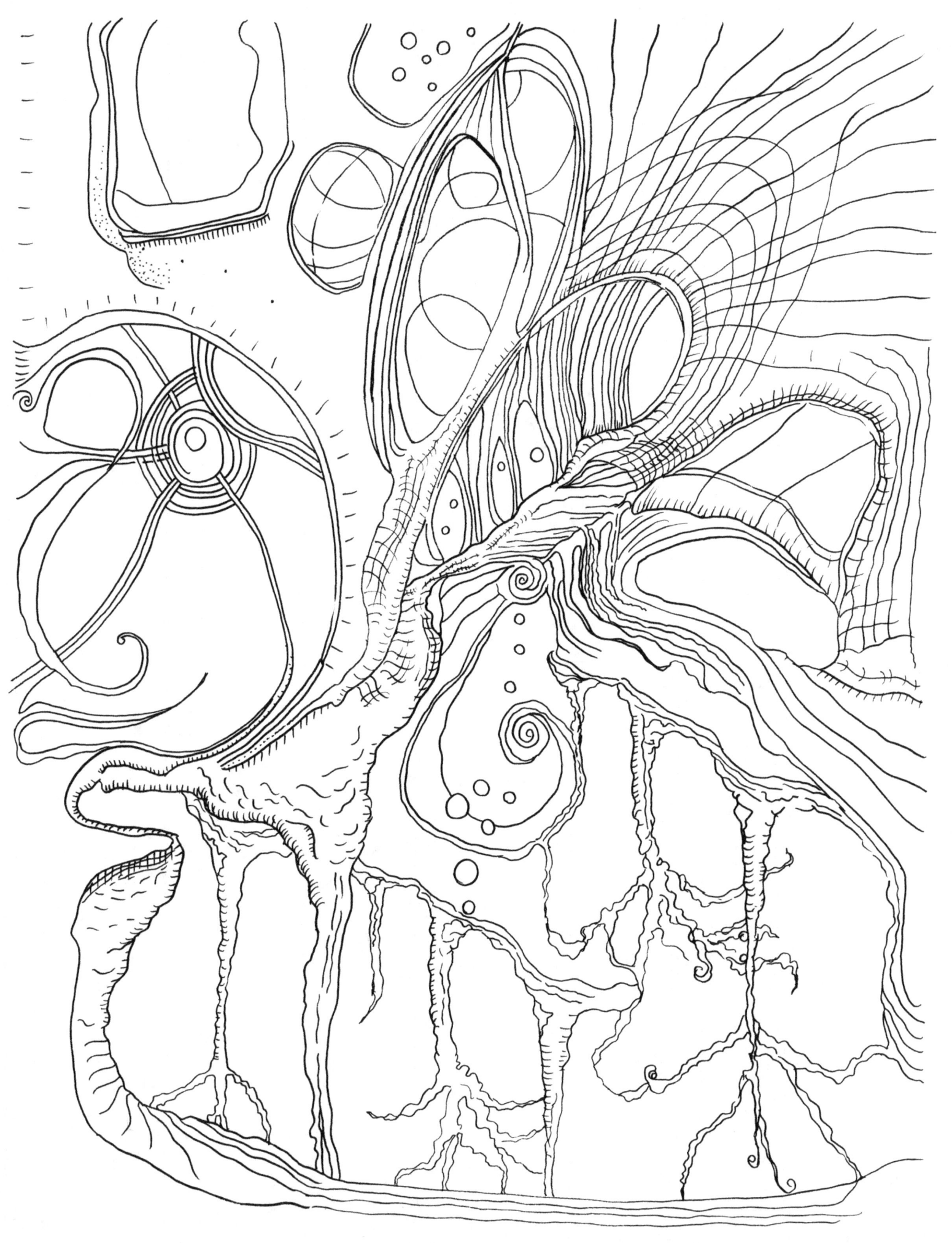

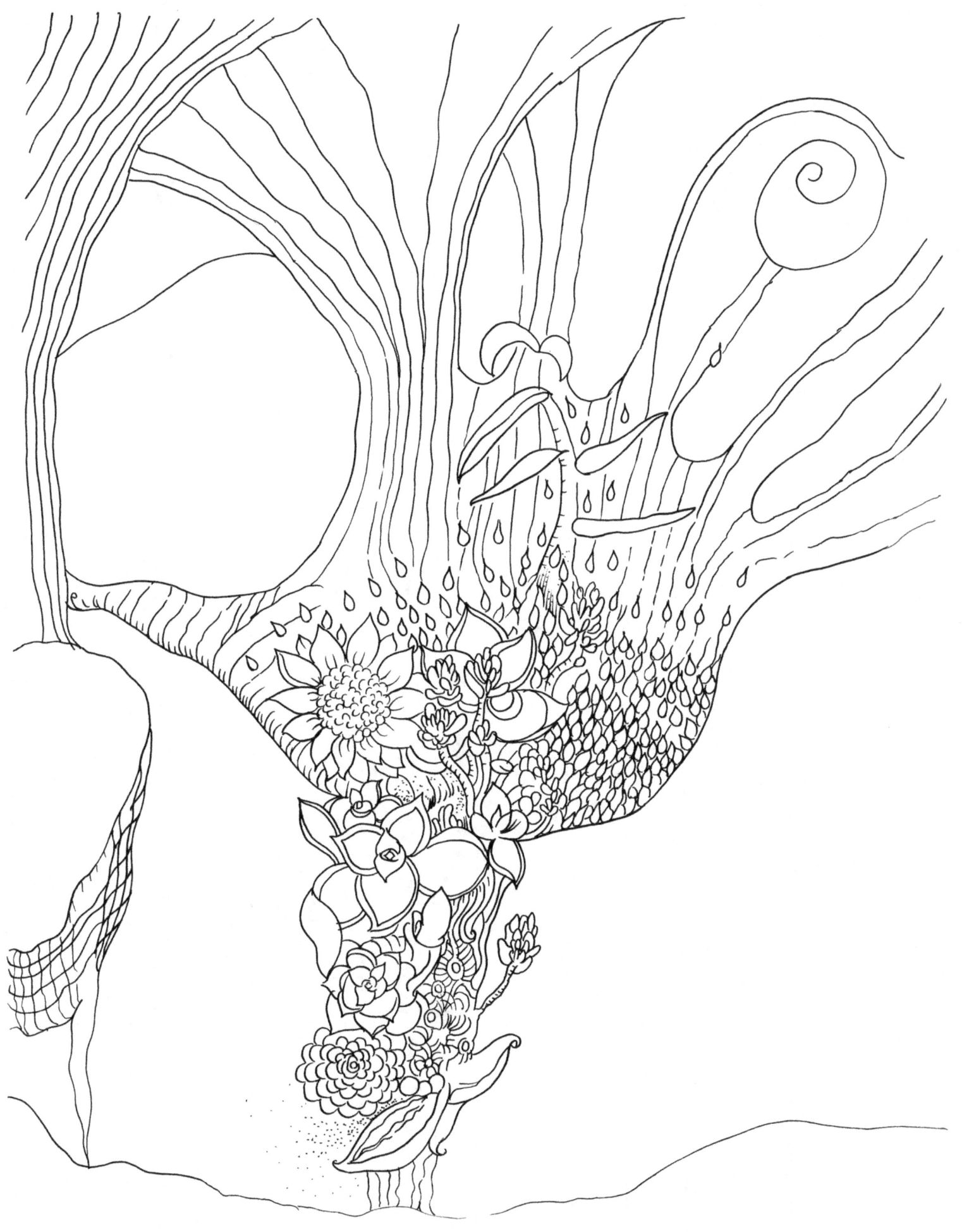

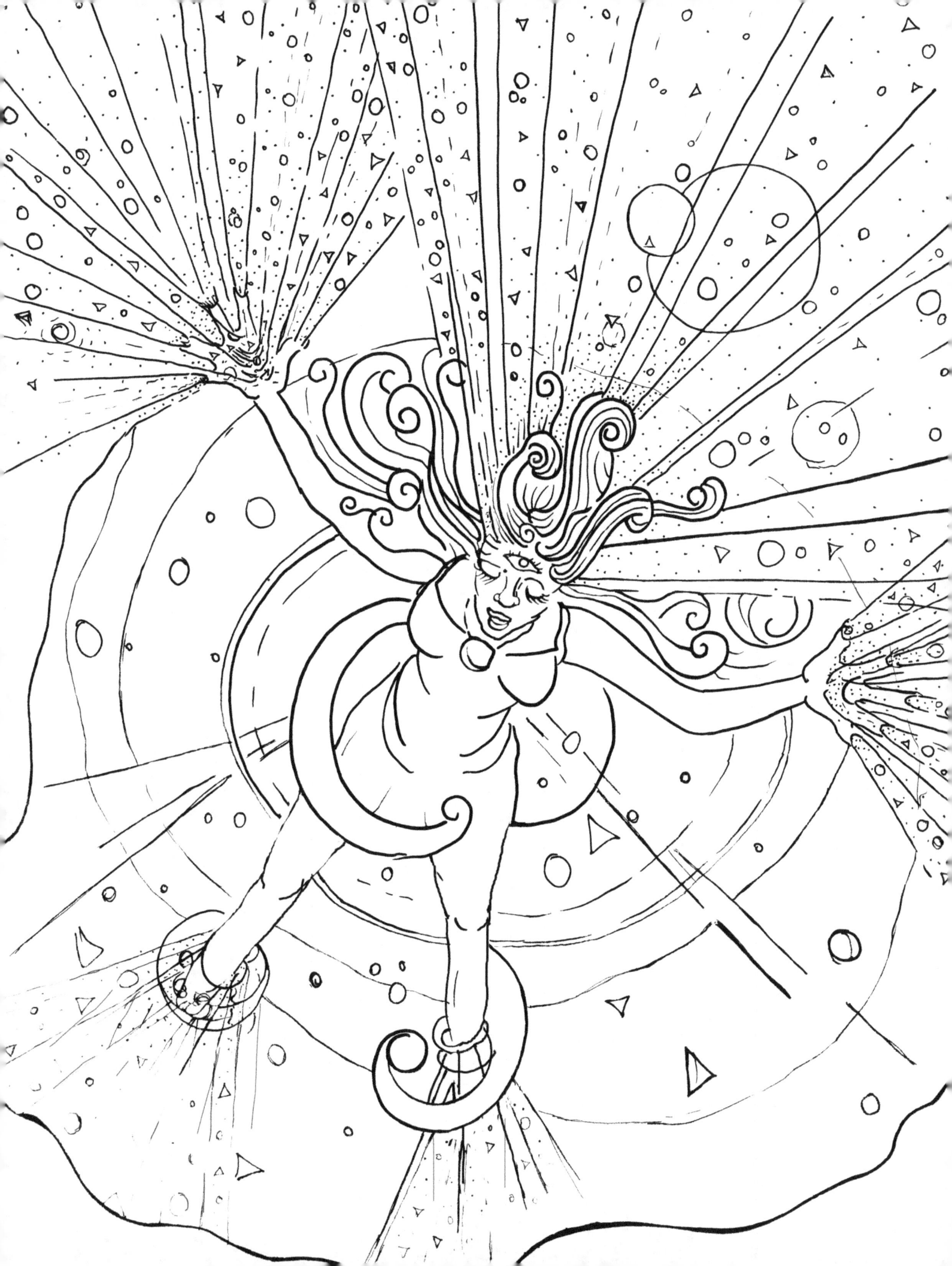

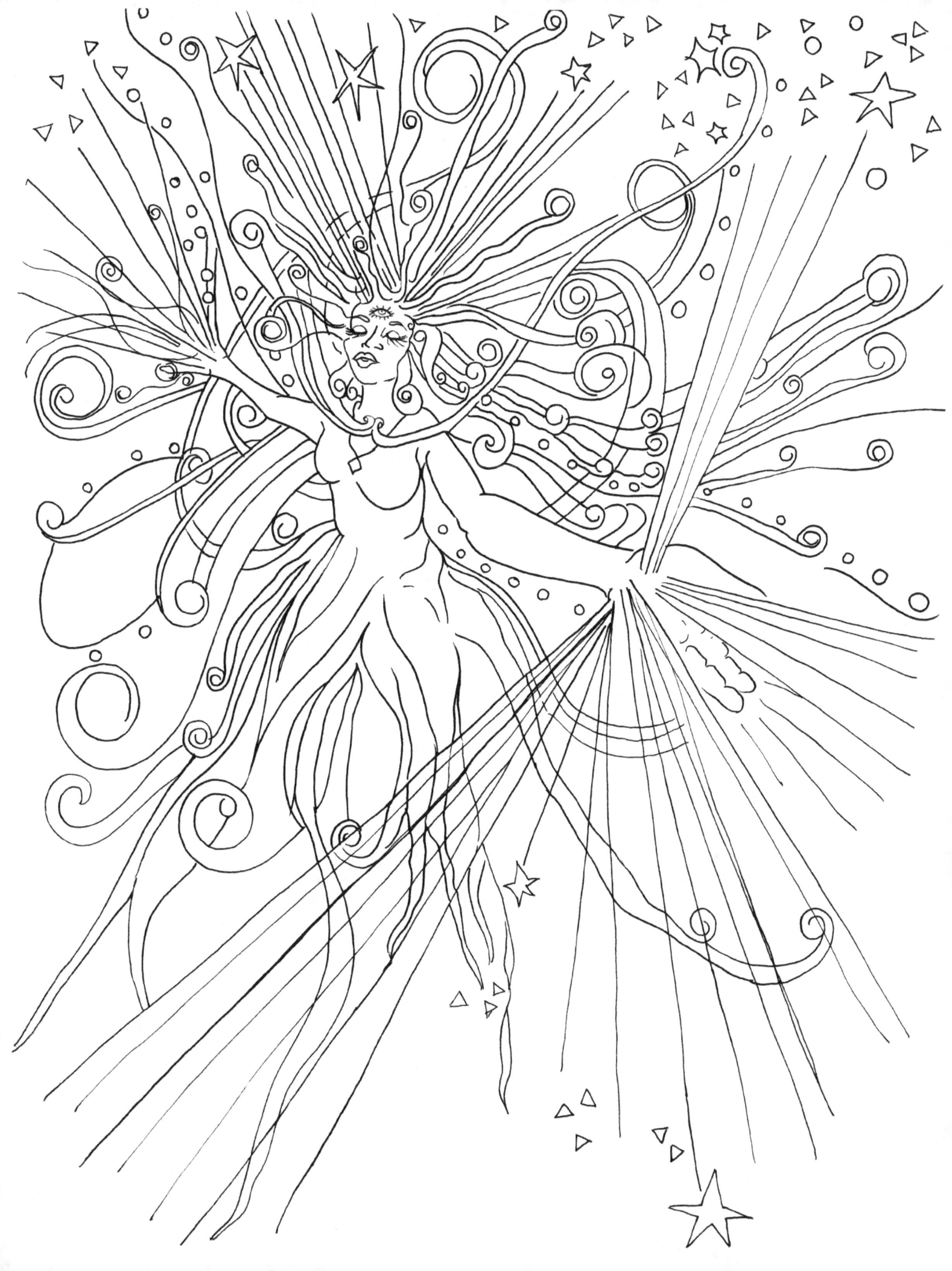

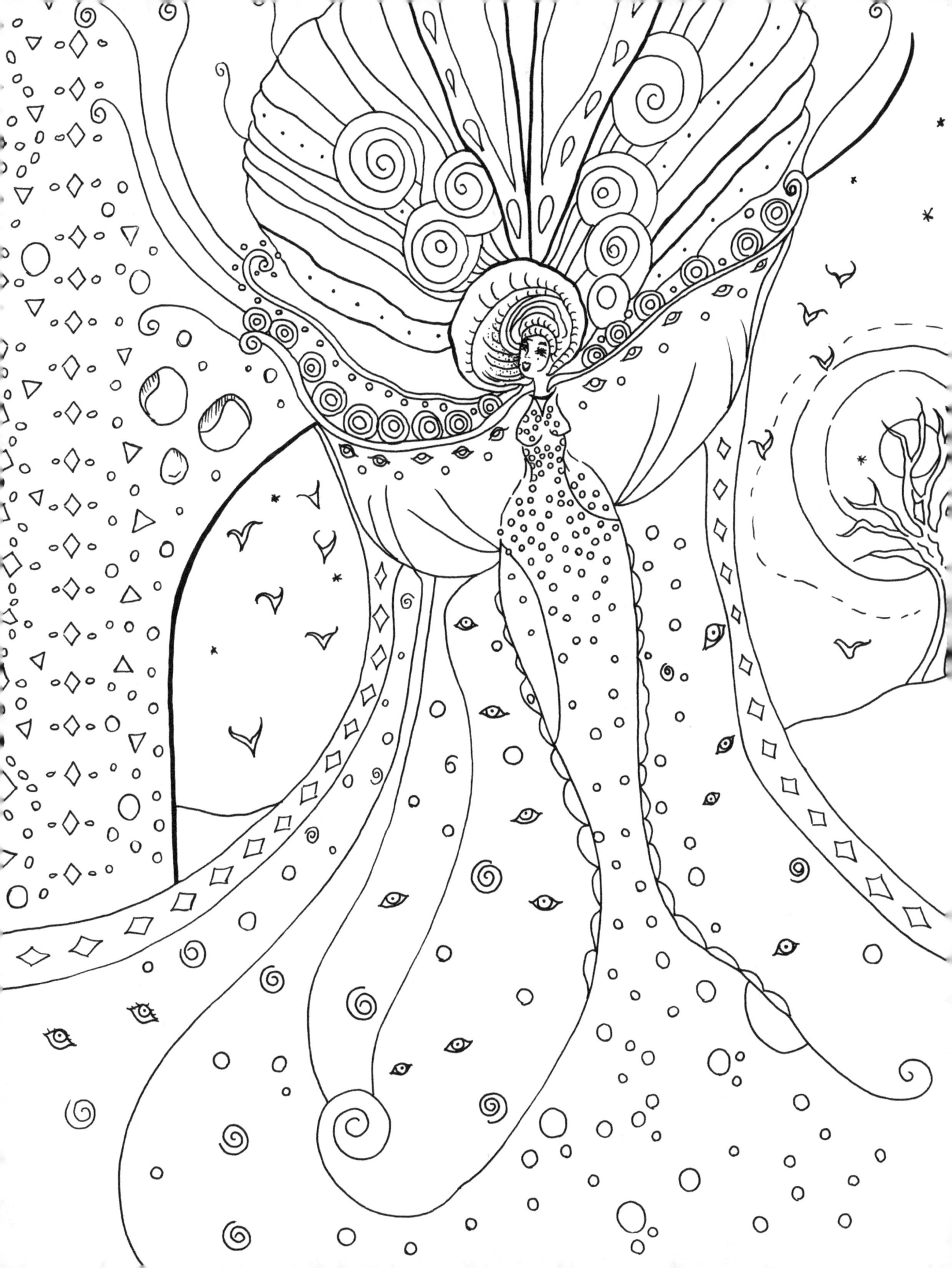

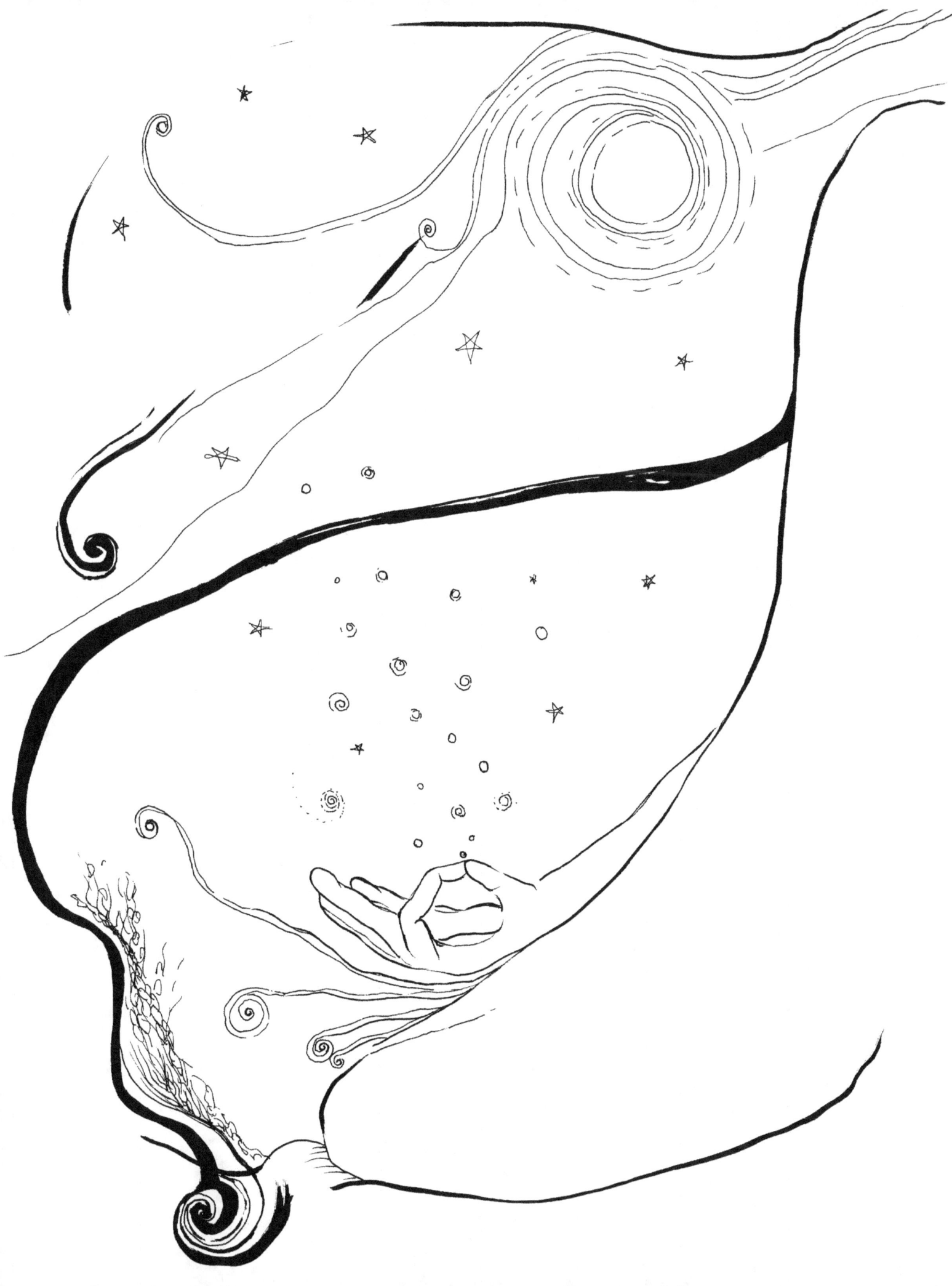

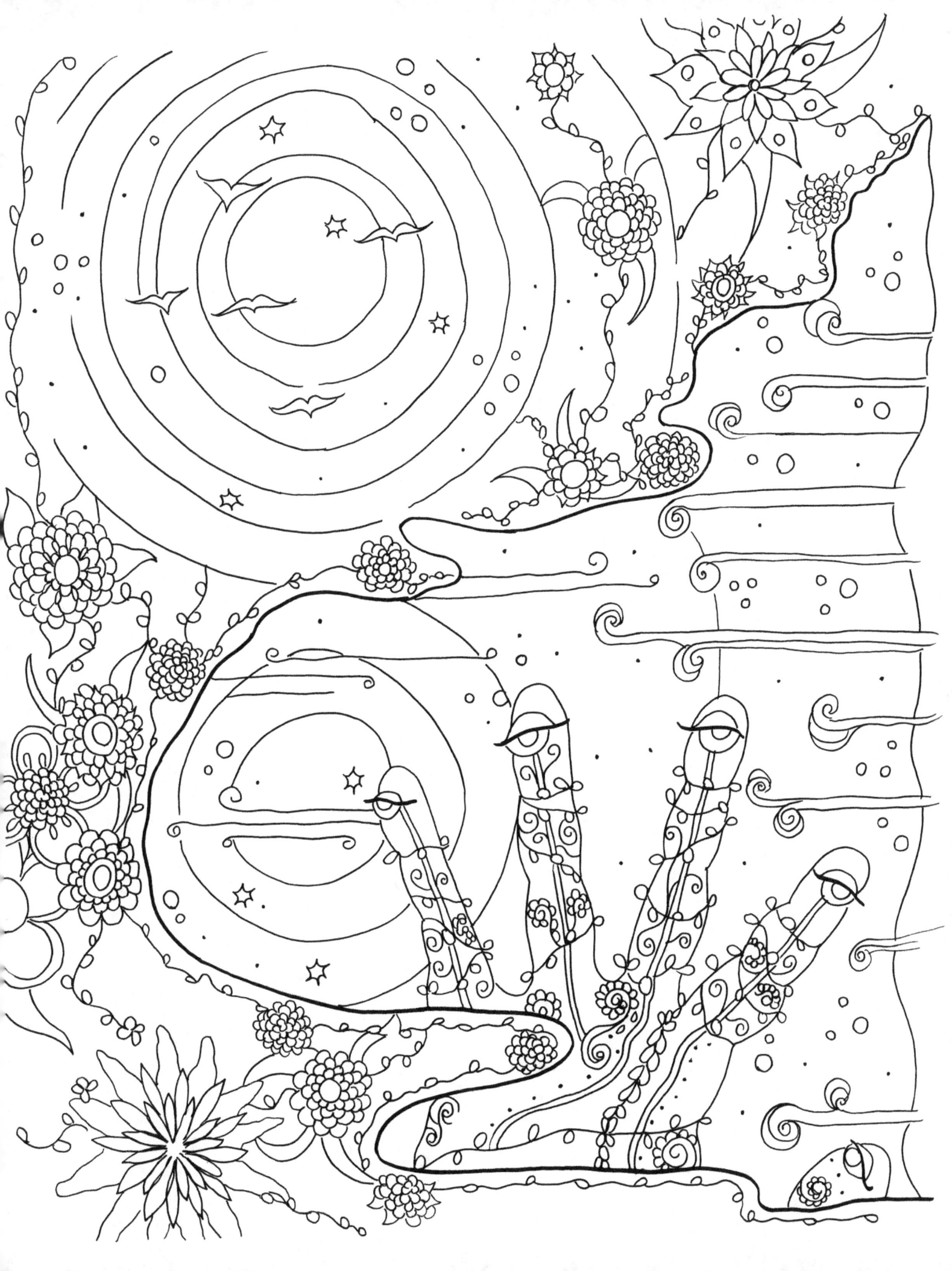

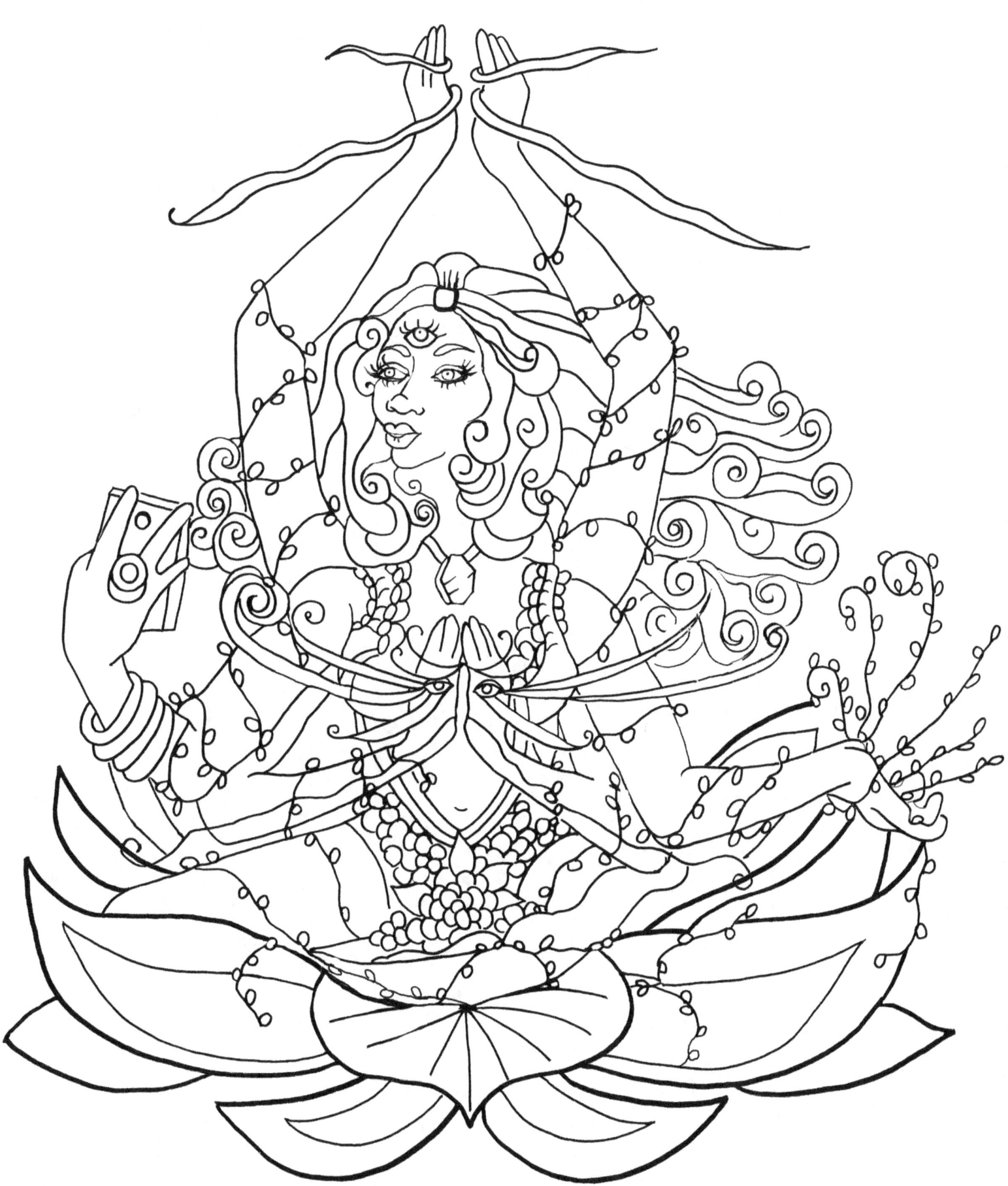

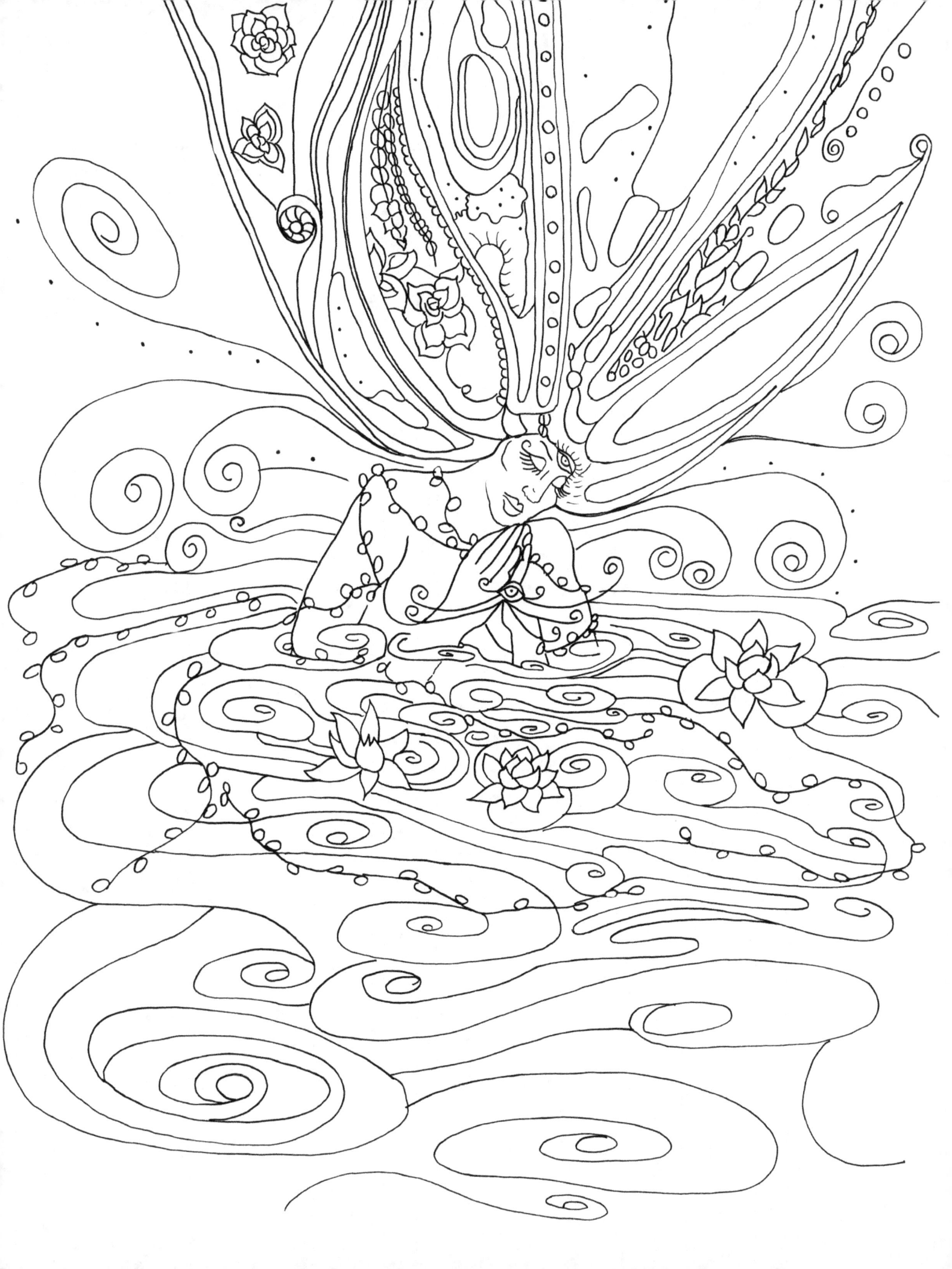

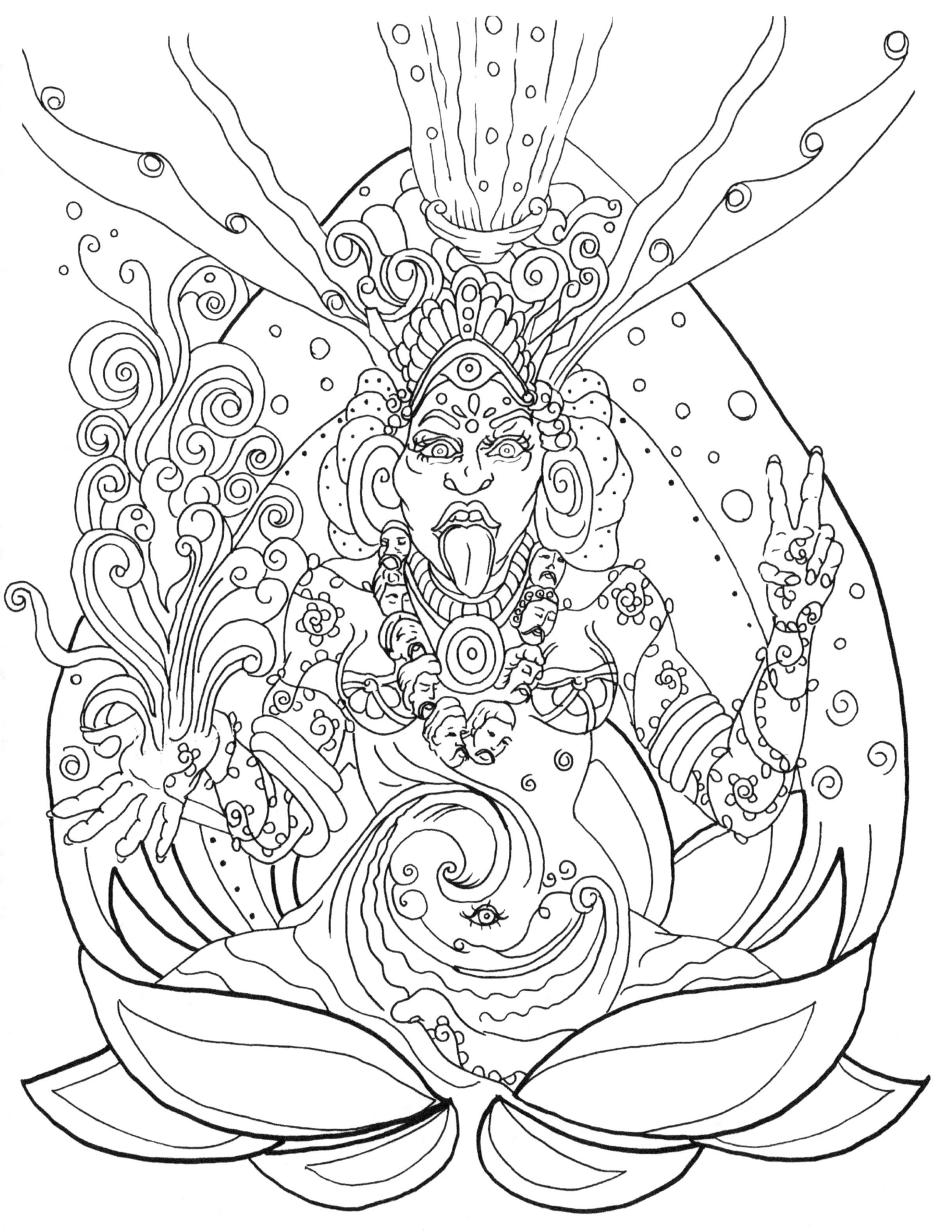

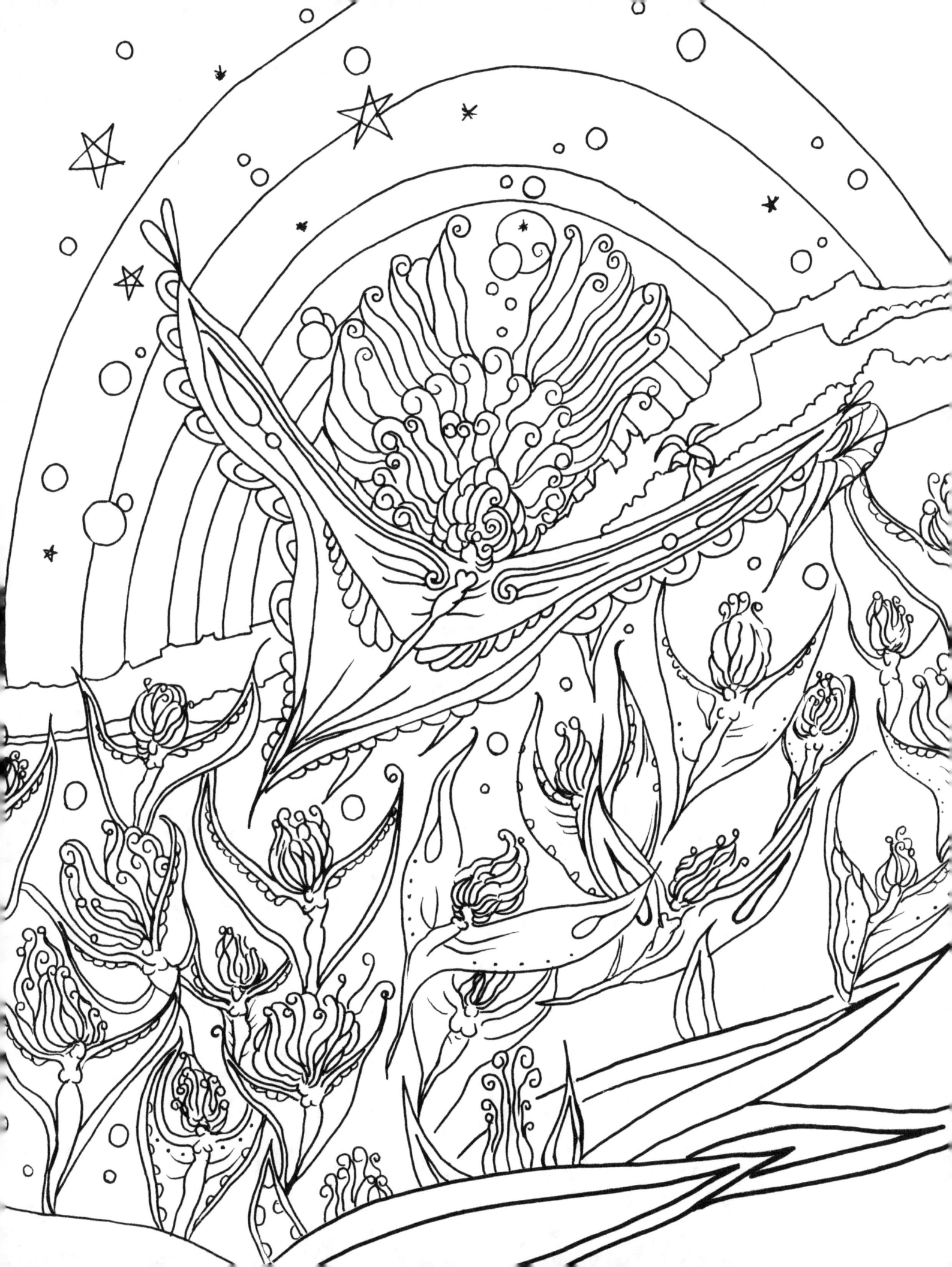

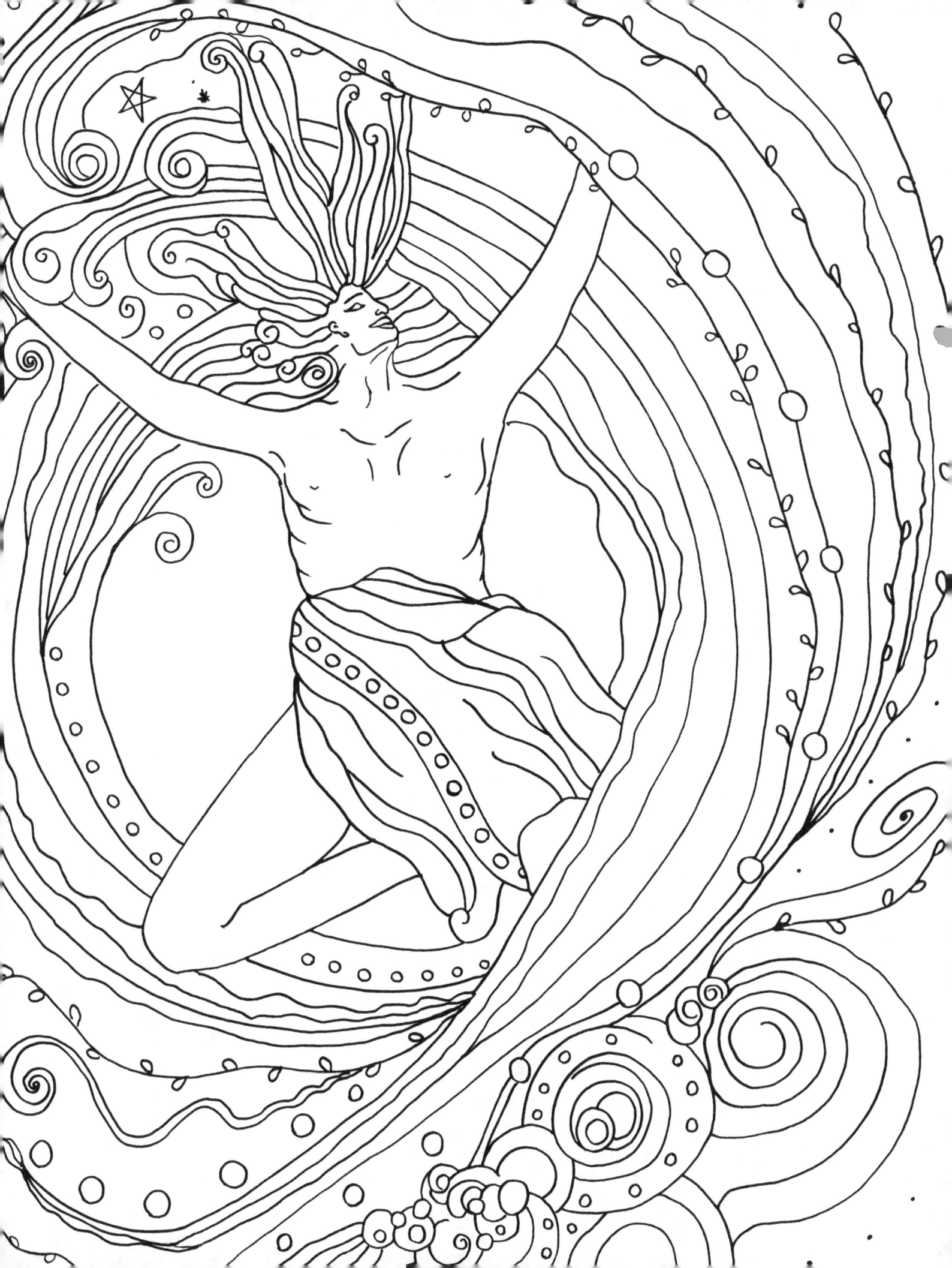

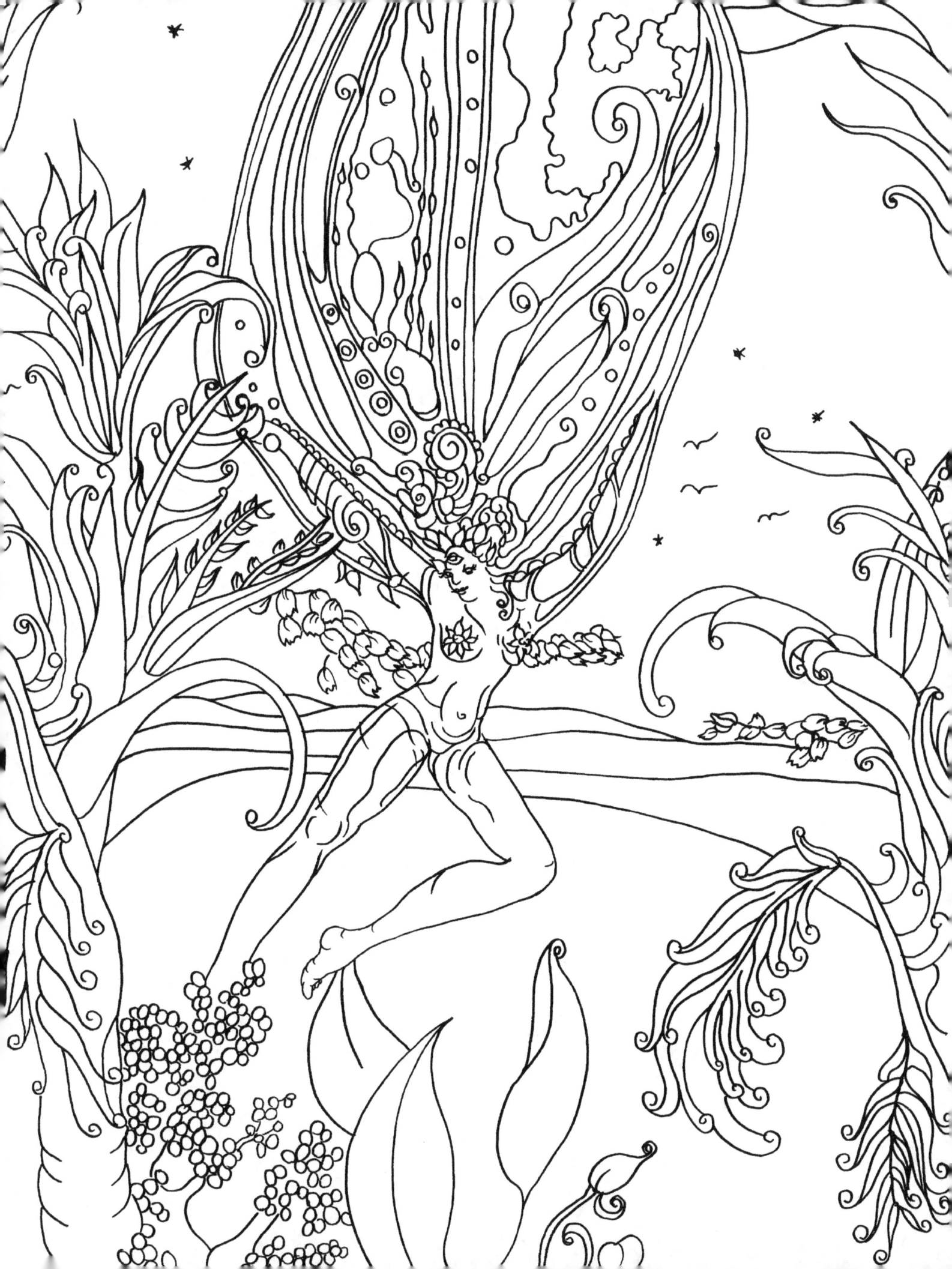

Valtopia: Your Guide

Calling on Durga Power

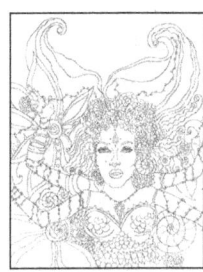

Rise above negative energies and call upon your invincibility. Like the literal translation of the word, you are a fort and force that cannot be overcome. Call upon the goddess, Durga, and her many tools to overcome the different obstacles you are facing. Red is the color of Durga's dress, and it fortifies our base chakra and stirs up our survival instincts, the sense of our own power and independence. It is a call to action, a battle cry, exciting and raising our enthusiasm and giving us energy. This brings us self-confidence built on fearless action without hesitation or self-doubt. Feel this power as you color and look at where you will rise up in your own life!

Crystal: Red jasper, tiger eye, garnet
Essential Oil: Melaleuca—Melaleuca is a disinfectant by nature that will empower you to you release old ties, negative baggage and toxic relationships. You will be FREE to create nurturing relationships and set upon your path with confidence.

Sacred Circle

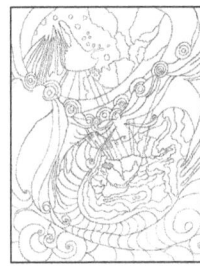

Imagine yourself connected hand-to-hand, open to receive and to send to all those in your sacred circle. A beautiful golden white column of light connects from above, as you call in all of your spirit guides, soul team and ascended masters. Feel the energy grow and circle above, about and around the sacred circle and feel the glorious connection and know that you are filled with love and purpose. Feel the love and light of the sacred circle as you color.

Crystal: Rose quartz, selenite and turquoise
Essential Oil: Wintergreen

You Are What You Think You Are

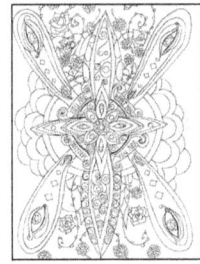

Our thoughts are extremely powerful. What we think affects how we feel, and how we feel is the energy we create. The energy we create is our experience of life. As you color this mandala, spin it every so often and repeat a beautiful affirmation for yourself. You are vibrant, vulnerable and vital. I love you.

Crystal: Rainbow fluorite, sodalite
Essential Oil: Lemon—Lemon is the oil of focus. It nourishes the mind and supports positive emotions. Enjoy the present moment with a joyful heart and an jubilant step as you enjoy an assist from lemon.

I Put My Ego and My Critical Mind Aside

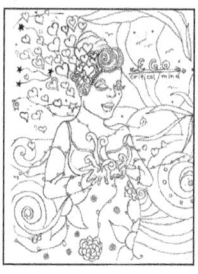

Say out loud, "I put my ego and my critical mind aside, and allow my subconscious and conscious mind to connect." Doing so allows your brain to put aside fear steeped in past history that has served to protect you, and opens up your mind and heart to all the creative, expansive, and powerful ideas and wisdom just blossoming and ready for you. Then color with abandon.

Crystal: Amethyst, howlite, snowflake obsidian
Essential Oil: Frankincense

Let Go

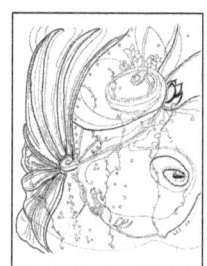

You must release the old, negative fears and ways in order to grow and expand into your most authentic, soaring self. Once you deeply acknowledge these fears and pains and find the cause and roots, thank and forgivingly release them so you may create new beliefs that are inspired and powerful and true. Ask for help in letting go. This is a most powerful step to creating your own empowerment and joy. As you color, let it all gooooo.

Crystal: Smoky and rutilated quartz, shungite, charoite
Essential Oil: Lemongrass—Lemongrass is known as the oil of cleansing. Allow lemongrass to help rid you of any feelings of despair, despondency limiting beliefs and old toxic energy. Lemongrass can teach you how to move forward on your path with confidence and joy.

Dream

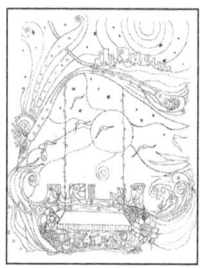

You must make time to envision and really feel into your heart's greatest desires and passion. These indicate that to which you are most attuned. Write them down, shape them, and create a reality guided by your dreams. When you follow your dreams, your passion is ignited and this lights you up and you shine in the universal light and flow and allow the rest of us to dream too. While you color, allow your wildest dreams with no judgement.

Crystal: Labradorite, astrophylite
Essential Oil: Ylang ylang—Often called the oil of the inner child, ylang ylang will open your heart and connect you to the spirit of your dreams.

Everything Is Everything

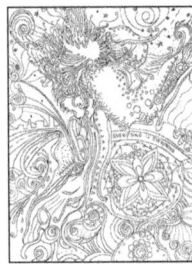

We are one, all interconnected. The air I breathe, you breathe. The water I drink, you drink. We look at the same sun and moon and stars, and energetically we are all interwoven. Make a choice and seek that which brings you up to your highest, most loving vibration. We all affect and create the reality we live. Feel into the interconnectedness of our earth, our galaxies, our universe, ourselves. Everything is everything.

Crystal: Apophylite, celestite, larimar
Essential Oil: Marjoram—Marjoram is the oil of connection. Marjoram will help you drop the barriers you build for protection and help you to trust so you may fully be yourself in all situations.

Self-Love

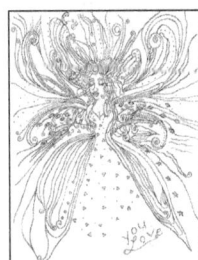

You have one most important gift and job, and only you can do this best. Love yourself and take care of yourself. The more you do loving and caring actions for yourself, the better you feel, the better your energy, and thus you radiate positivity and love that comes right from source—from you. Your self-love is truly universal love and we can feel when you love yourself and allow your light to shine. Feel that love as you color and know that you are taking wonderful steps to care for you.

Crystal: Rose quartz, pink kunzite, rhodonite, morganite and pink danburite
Essential Oil: Bergamot—Bergamot is the oil of self-acceptance. It will awaken your soul to hope and encourage you to share your inner self.

We Are Connected

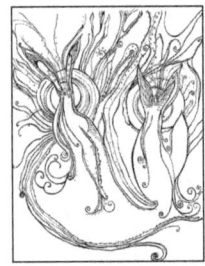

When we open up and ask to receive, and we have cared for ourselves with love, we are able to open up to the love of the universe. All the energy of the galaxies and universe are connected, like a big wave, and our connection ripples throughout our experience. As you color, know and feel into that connection and feel the universal love, guidance and acceptance.

Crystal: Danburite, aquamarine, green prehnite
Essential Oil: Marjoram—Marjoram is the oil of connection. Marjoram will help you drop the barriers you build for protection and help you to trust, so you may fully be yourself in all situations.

New Roots

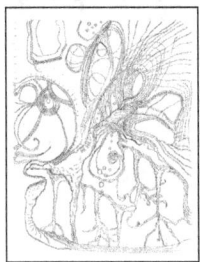

When we release the old, digging up the roots of fears and pains of the past, we create the fertile space for fresh intentions, dreams and manifestations. From your dreams, allow new roots of expansive visions to flourish and grow. As you color, water your seeds with your mind, feeling into them and nurturing and encouraging growth.

Crystal: Pyrite, carnelian, green tourmaline
Essential Oil: Oregano—Release old attachments and negativity with the powerful help of oregano. Oregano encourages true freedom from the past and a deeper connection to your soul.

Blossoming

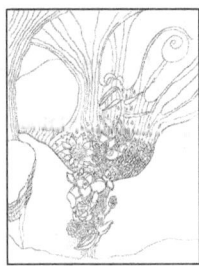

Like a spring garden, once you have watered and nurtured the seeds of intention, your heart and spirit flourishes, blossoming into new beginnings. Anything is possible! Let your beautiful self blossom and thrive. As you color, delight in the new blooming of you and your baby sprouts as they burst into the light of day.

Crystal: Orange calcite, coral, green aventurine
Essential Oil: Geranium—Geranium is the oil of love and trust. Geranium will restore your confidence in the innate goodness of yourself and the world, so you can blossom with love and confidence.

Shine, Baby, Shine!

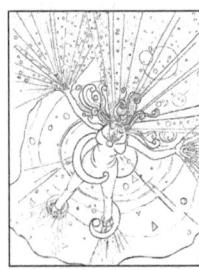

Now you are flourishing and radiant. Your light bright and shining like a beacon, there's no faking this one. When you're here you'll know, because everyone will tell you so and you'll feel glorious. Love it, embody it and shine, baby, shine! Feel yourself shine as you color.

Crystal: Sunstone, citrine
Essential Oil: Lavender—Lavender addresses the fear of being seen and heard. Lavender helps you express your true self, to be seen, to be heard, to share the true essence of who you really are.

Take Flight

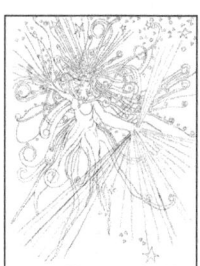

You are clear, connected and conscious. You know how to ask and to receive and in your beautiful faith and belief, you take flight in your heart and your spirit. You have no fear and taking the leap, you fly effortlessly. Feel that faith and fly with confidence as you color.

Crystal: Imperial topaz, ametrine
Essential Oil: Peppermint—Peppermint is the oil of a joyous heart. Peppermint will invigorate your body, mind and spirit, reminding you that there is nothing to fear.

Super-Moon Manifestation

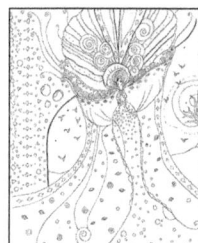

The moon is such a powerful force in our co-creation of experience. There are so many lovely rituals you can perform at each turn of the moon cycles. Use these forceful energies to release the old, and set intentions for the new. Watch your life miraculously evolve as you dream it up. Feel it and believe it with super-moon manifestation magic while you color.

Crystal: Moonstone, quartz, obsidian, amethyst
Essential Oil: Sandalwood— Sandalwood assists with prayer, meditation and spirituality. Its powerful ability to calm the mind, still the heart and connect with your higher self will allow you to truly step into your creative power.

Meditation

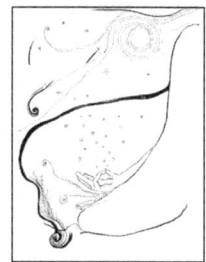

In these moments when you sit quietly with yourself, thinking of nothing, hearing your own breath, or listening to that music or guided meditation, it allows you to go within and still the worry, quiet the racket, and clear the way to really listen and receive your own inner intuitive guidance. This drawing is intentionally open and expansive. Color it in with the big patches of color or draw your own ideas that allow you to relax and contemplate and be.

Crystal: Labradorite, fluorite, aquamarine, quartz
Essential Oil: Sandalwood—Sandalwood assists with prayer, meditation and spirituality. Its powerful ability to calm the mind, still the heart and connect with your higher self will allow you to truly step into your creative power.

Bodhi Tree

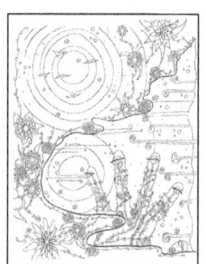

It is under the bodhi tree that the Buddha is said to have attained enlightenment. It is known as the wisdom tree, and has, throughout history, represented the individual's journey to infinity and awakening. I drew this near the bodhi tree at the Pepper Tree Inn in Ojai, California, the former home of Krishnamurti. As you color this page, know that you are on your own path towards your own beautiful shining light within.

Crystal: Jade and agate
Essential Oil: Rosemary—Rosemary teaches us that there is a greater wisdom than the mind. Dive deep within yourself with the help of rosemary. Connect with your intuition and receive inspired answers.

Golden Goddess

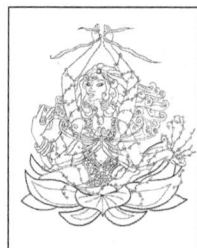

I am expanding my energy daily to receive greater abundance. I am golden love and light and radiate gorgeous energy that illuminates and vitalizes, because I love and appreciate myself daily.

Crystal: Lapis, shunghite, selenite
Essential Oil: Myrrh—Like the warmth of a mother's love for her child, myrrh will assist you to feel safe, secure and nurtured.

Gratitude

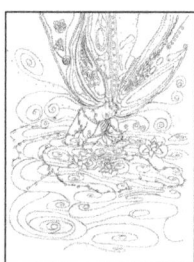

There is nothing more powerful and magical than truly feeling deep gratitude, when you really feel into all that you have and are, and come into a positive state of thankfulness. Your energy flows and you're able to receive fully, recognizing the abundance that already surrounds you. No matter what your circumstances, this allows you to shift into a beautiful state of mind. Color this and think of all the things that fill you with gratitude.

Crystal: Rose quartz, pink danburite
Essential Oil: Orange—Orange is the oil of abundance. Allow orange to inspire abundance, support a positive attitude, and restore and rejuvenate you. Orange teaches you to let go of a scarcity mindset and step into the limitless supply nature constantly offers us.

Kali Babe Power

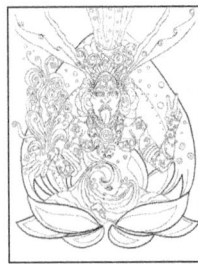

From the Indian goddess, Kali, we draw fierce and fiery power. We draw up the strength to "lose it" and thrash that which no longer serves or works and shake everything up until we can begin anew and some order and balance has been restored. This representation only evokes some of the visual symbols she normally possesses, but is imbued with all of that potent, life-changing energy. Summon up your feisty Kali babe while you color this in and rock your world!

Crystal: Obsidian, fire agate, charoite
Essential Oil: Clove—Clove gives you the power to say no and create boundaries. It reignites the inner fire of your soul and allows you to stand up and clearly articulate your needs and desires.

Angel Sisters

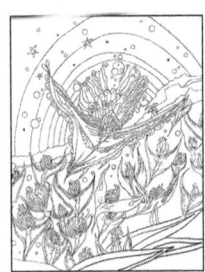

Without my angel sisters none of these concepts would have been so deeply absorbed and my transformation so rapid. Find your sacred circle of sisters and connections that enable your inspiration, your support and your thriving expansion. These connections are vital and nourishing. You can find them virtually online and in person. While you color, either thank the support you have or ask to receive some wonderful angel sisters. Thank you, angel sisters!

Crystal: Chrysocolla, larimar, moonstone
Essential Oil: Cedarwood—Cedarwood is the oil of community. Cedarwood will remind you that you are not alone. It invites you to give and receive, so you may thrive with the support of groups and fully experience the joy of relationships.

Flow

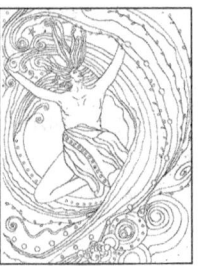

When you have explored and released your past, felt in the gratitude, and allowed yourself to believe and receive, when you have gone into yourself with quiet meditation and are tuned into your own intuition and guidance and are connected spiritually and universally, you experience a grace and ease of alignment. This alignment is your spirit connected to its highest desire and purpose that clicks into the whole of us. It's a beautiful energy where everything is in flow.

Crystal: Rose quartz, ametrine, turquoise
Essential Oil: Sandalwood—Sandalwood assists with prayer, meditation and spirituality. Its powerful ability to calm the mind, still the heart and connect with your higher self will allow you to truly step into your creative power.

Bliss

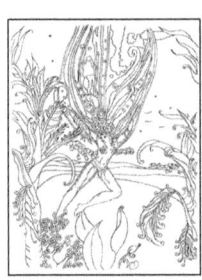

Utter release, metamorphosis, full faith, light shining brightly, you are evolved from a place of stagnancy to fluid energetic brilliance. You are expansive and enlightened, reveling in a gorgeous loving state of bliss. Enjoy the beauty that lies within and without. Blessings and joy as you color your bliss.

Crystal: Sapphire, citrine, angel aura quartz
Essential Oil: Rose—Rose oil holds the highest frequency of essential oils. It will help you embody divine love and help restore your authenticity, wholeness and purity.

*Hearfelt thanks to Becky Kimes for the essential oils,
and to Asha Milkowski for the crystals.*

Join Valtopia on Facebook at *www.facebook.com/groups/Valtopia/* to follow Val and to connect with others on their spiritual and creative journeys.